HER MAJESTY'S
ROYAL PALACE AND FORTRESS
OF THE
TOWER *of* LONDON

PETER HAMMOND

Designed by Trickett and Webb Limited

Cover illustrations by Glynn Boyd Harte

Centre pages illustration by Don Pottinger MA (Hons) DA

CONTENTS

---❖---

THE MAKING *of* THE TOWER

THE BUILDINGS *of* THE TOWER

THE ROYAL ARMOURIES

THE CROWN JEWELS

THE COMMUNITY *of* THE TOWER

---❖---

A perspective view of the Tower appears on the centre pages

THE MAKING *of* THE TOWER

FORTRESS AND PALACE

❖

The First Castle

On Christmas Day 1066 William Duke of Normandy was crowned King of England in Westminster Abbey, some two months after his victory over the Saxon King Harold at Hastings. At once William ordered the building of fortifications to help secure London, the chief city of his new kingdom. One of these earth-and-timber castles was erected in the south-east corner of the Roman city walls, to command the River Thames as well as the city. To close off the angle between the walls and complete the bailey, or yard, of the new castle, the Normans made a ditch and bank surmounted by a palisade.

Ten years later, by then in full control of England, William determined to transform this simple fort into a massive palace-fortress. A great stone tower was built and at once entitled the Tower of London. Later, as the castle was enlarged around it, that name was to be given to the entire fortress, and the great central tower became known as the White Tower.

William the Conqueror, depicted on the Bayeux Tapestry. The building beside him may be the great tower of the Dukes of Normandy at Rouen, built in the tenth century and demolished in 1204. This was perhaps the model for the White Tower which William certainly saw as the counterpart of the castle at Rouen – a fortified palace dominating the chief city of his new lands.

After nine hundred years William the Conqueror's palace-fortress, the White Tower, still dominates the Tower of London.

Key to the four dated plans

Building existing before this period

New building in this period

▪▪▪▪▪▪
Conjectural new building in this period

Outline of the present Tower buildings

For a century the Tower of London begun by the Conqueror and completed by his son, William Rufus, remained unchanged. Then, between 1190 and 1285, the White Tower was encircled by two towered curtain walls and a great moat. The only important enlargement of the Tower after that time was the building of the wharf, which continued up to about 1400. To this day the medieval defences are essentially unchanged, except at the main entrance, on the west side.

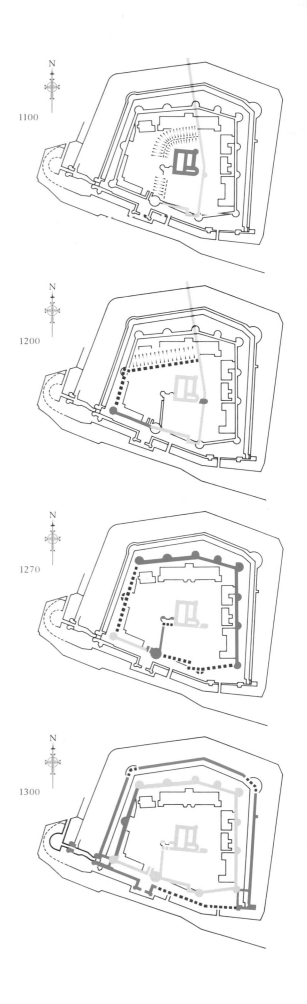

The Castle Enlarged

In 1189, while Richard I, the Lionheart, was away on crusade, his chancellor William Longchamp, Bishop of Ely, began the first expansion of the Tower's defences. It was completed by Richard's brother John, who succeeded him in 1199. The bailey around the White Tower was almost doubled in area, and fortified with a new curtain wall and towers, and with a ditch beyond. Even so the Londoners were not to be deterred from joining John's enemies among the barons, and the King, having lost the city, had to agree to Magna Carta in 1215.

The Castle Transformed

The making of a knight in the White Tower as depicted in Writhe's Garter Book. After the ritual bath he would keep vigil throughout the night, and the next day would receive the sword and spurs of knighthood from the king.

John's son, Henry III (1216-72), at first gave his attention to improving the Tower as a royal residence. Within the space between the White Tower and the river a splendid new palace took shape, supplanting the royal accommodation within the White Tower itself. As one of the palace amusements, Henry established a royal menagerie.

When Henry's lofty view of kingship brought him into dispute with his barons, he ordered a massive expansion of the Tower's defences. The area of the castle was again doubled, this time being extended on all three landward sides so that the White Tower now stood at its centre. The new curtain wall around the enlarged bailey was guarded by towers at regular intervals, and by a wide moat. Even then, Henry, like his father, had to submit for a time to an alliance of the Londoners and hostile barons and to surrender the Tower.

The Castle Completed

Henry's son Edward I (1272-1307) came to the throne determined to master the turbulent city. In ten years, between 1275 and 1285, he spent twice as much on the Tower as his father had done during his entire reign. A new moat was excavated, a new curtain wall was built along its edge, and Henry III's moat was filled in. A towered curtain wall was constructed along the river foreshore containing new royal accommodation, and the ground behind was built up. Edward paid particular attention to the elaborate fortification of the new landward entrance, across the moat.

The Tower, with its moat, now extended over 18 acres (7.3 ha), and nothing was lacking to make it an impregnable fortress except that, as in earlier times, the readiness of the defenders to fight still mattered more than the strength of the defences. This was to be strikingly shown during the Peasants' Revolt of 1381

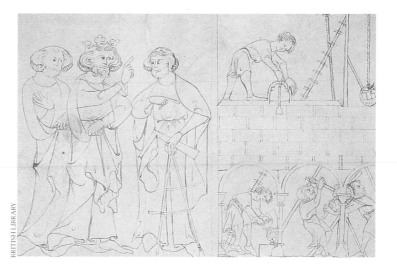

Henry III instructs his masons, as shown in a contemporary drawing. Henry loved fine buildings and rich decoration and spent lavishly at the Tower as well as at his many other residences. His architects also transformed the Tower's defences.

Edward I, son of Henry III, holds court, as depicted by a contemporary artist. While not neglecting royal splendour, Edward was dedicated to war and government, rather than to the arts and piety as his father had been. He made the Tower into one of the great castles of the age.

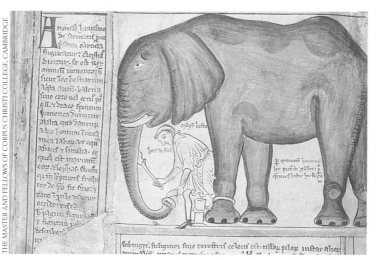

Henry III's elephant, presented to him by King Louis of France in 1255, and kept at the Tower. Henry also sent there three leopards given to him by the German Emperor, and a polar bear which had been presented by the King of Norway.

when, after the young Richard II had left the Tower to negotiate with some of the rebels, others appeared demanding entry. The garrison dared not resist and put the King at risk, and an exuberant crowd swept in, seeking loot and revenge. Again, in 1460 during the Wars of the Roses, after the Tower had been besieged and bombarded, the garrison preferred to surrender on conditions, rather than fight on in a lost cause.

ARSENAL, TREASURY AND MINT

A medieval castle, as well as being the stronghold and residence of its lord, was also the place that held his treasure, armoury and prisoners. The Tower, as a great royal castle adjoining London, the commercial capital, and near Westminster, which had become the seat of government, was a major centre of the power and wealth of English monarchs.

Following Edward I's expansion of the Tower, it soon came to contain one of the main royal treasuries, a storehouse for official documents, the largest of the royal mints and the only one coining in gold as well as silver, and the chief arsenal in the kingdom, storing and assembling armaments for the royal armies and fleets. To speed the movement of supplies and afford storage and working space, the wharf was extended along the entire river front.

The Tower played a major role in Edward III's successes against the French, as arsenal and mint. This gold noble celebrates the naval victory of Sluys in 1340.

Richard II, at the age of 14, displayed astonishing courage during the Peasants' Revolt. Eighteen years later he became the first English king to be imprisoned in the Tower. This contemporary portrait is in Westminster Abbey.

STATE PRISON

In medieval times the Tower also found room for prisoners who in one way or another were accounted the king's enemies, ranging from rioting London apprentices to foreign monarchs and nobles captured in war.

From the later years of Henry VIII's reign (1509-47) the Tower gradually went out of use as a royal palace as Whitehall became the monarch's usual London residence, and the Tower's defences were allowed to decay. The expanding operations of the arsenal and the mint came to dominate Tower life, along with the ever-growing number of prisoners of state, the victims of court rivalries, dynastic disputes and religious animosities.

Of the many hundreds of prisoners brought to the Tower, a small number were kept in deliberately harsh conditions and put to the torture. They, and a larger number who were spared such horrors, left the Tower only to suffer a traitor's death. The great majority of men and women held there were sooner or later released, and stories of innumerable prisoners suffering in deep dungeons and torture chambers are mostly the inventions of propagandists at the time or romantic novelists of a later age.

ROYAL ARMOURIES

It was in the reign of the ruthless, self-righteous Henry VIII that the Tower became known above all as the chief prison of state.

The pre-coronation procession of Edward VI, the nine-year-old son of Henry VIII, leaves the Tower to pass through London to Westminster. From Richard II, in 1377, to Charles II, in 1661, almost every new sovereign came to the Tower before coronation.

THE TOWER OF LONDON.
circa 1689.

This view, by Johannes Spilberg, about 1689, shows the Tower as both a fashionable place of resort and a renovated fortress bristling with cannon. During a major overhaul of the defences, in 1683, a series of gun platforms had been built, some on top of the medieval towers which were now capped with parapets of brick. Overtopping even the White Tower is the newly completed Grand Storehouse, which held arms and equipment for an entire army. The partly demolished wall in the foreground of the picture had been part of a defensive outwork around the main entrance. The gateway beyond the wooden fence, on the right of the picture, led straight to the menagerie, one of the Tower's chief public attractions.

GARRISON AND SHOWPLACE

Following the restoration of the monarchy in 1660, with the return from exile of Charles II, the Tower underwent major renovation, with substantial changes to its buildings and character. To ensure that the new King should never lose control of London, as his father Charles I had done on the eve of the Civil War, a large permanent garrison was housed in the Tower and batteries of guns set in place along the walls, while the arsenal, by then under the control of the Board of Ordnance, was expanded. Soon the coronation regalia were put on public show at the Tower, and the historic arms and armour, as well as parts of the new arsenal, were arranged in spectacular exhibitions calculated to impress sightseers with the strength and splendour of English monarchy. Meanwhile, the Tower remained the prison of state, though not much used except in national emergencies, such as the Jacobite Rebellions of 1715 and 1745 and the French Revolution; and it still accommodated the Royal Mint and state records.

A great fire at the Tower in 1841, which began with an overheated stove in the Bowyer Tower, completely destroyed the Grand Storehouse and its vast stocks of service weapons. It was the end of the Tower's 500 years as a national arsenal. For a time the fire threatened the White Tower, and the Crown Jewels were hurriedly removed from the Martin Tower nearby.

These diverse institutions and uses co-existed uneasily until the primacy of the Tower's military role was re-asserted following the appointment of the Duke of Wellington as Constable in 1826. Wellington, like many others at the time, believed England to be on the brink of revolution, and he saw the security and strength of the Tower as his first responsibility. Already the Royal Mint had moved out. Wellington had the menagerie closed and obtained agreement that the public records were to be removed. When the main Ordnance building, the Grand Storehouse, was destroyed by fire in 1841, it was replaced by a vast new barracks block. The defences were strengthened, and Wellington even urged, though in vain, that the sightseeing public should be excluded, as a threat to the Tower's security.

Following the restoration of Charles II, seen here in the coronation portrait by John Michael Wright, the Tower played an important part in renewing the strength and splendour of monarchy, as fortress, garrison, and showplace.

TOURISM AND TRADITION

By the time of Wellington's death in 1852, the fear of revolution had passed. For the first time in its history the Tower was no longer seen as a significant military presence that might help to subdue riot or rebellion in London. Instead, with the

A Yeoman Warder with visitors at the scaffold site on Tower Green in 1895. Even in Tudor times, when their main responsibility was the safekeeping of prisoners, the Yeoman Warders had acted as guides to the few privileged visitors who were occasionally admitted to the Tower. The dark blue-and-red undress uniform, the everyday wear of the Yeoman Warders, was introduced in 1858.

encouragement of Queen Victoria's husband, Prince Albert, the Tower began to take on the character of a national monument. Ordnance buildings which had replaced or obscured the historic fabric were gradually demolished, and the medieval walls and towers were restored or even totally re-created. At the end of Victoria's reign in 1901, half a million people visited the Tower each year, largely drawn by the romantic appeal of the darker side of its history as popularised in novels, paintings and engravings of the time. Nowadays, the number of visitors is about two million annually, three-quarters of them from overseas. The Tower has become one of the world's great tourist attractions. Nevertheless, it remains a community, as it has always been, and it is this continuing village life within the walls which links the present-day Tower to its long and eventful past, no less than its buildings, ceremonies and traditions.

The Duke of Wellington, Constable of the Tower between 1826 and 1852, set out to restore its military importance, and to remove anything which detracted from it, including the visiting public. Portrait by Alfred, Count d'Orsay.

THE BUILDINGS *of* THE TOWER

THE WHITE TOWER

Work began on the *White Tower* in or shortly before 1078, under the supervision of a Norman monk, Gundulf, Bishop of Rochester, and was probably not completed until 1097, ten years after the death of William the Conqueror.

As a palace-fortress, the White Tower was designed to accommodate both the king and the Constable of the Tower, or his deputy, who commanded the garrison. Each occupied a self-contained set of rooms, the Constable on the entrance floor, the monarch on the upper floor. Each floor contained a hall, for public occasions; a chamber, no doubt divided up into smaller apartments by wooden partitions; and a chapel. The royal suite, naturally on a grander scale, occupied the whole of the upper two storeys, the present top floor being inserted much later. The basement contained the storerooms and the well.

After a century or so, as the castle was enlarged, the Constable took up residence at a key point in the new defences while royalty moved to the new palace outside the White Tower. Even so, monarchs still worshipped in the royal chapel and in times of crisis the White Tower was a secure meeting place for the king's council and a refuge for the monarch himself.

At other times, the royal apartments might be occupied by distinguished prisoners. The first, in 1100, shortly after the building was completed, was Ranulf Flambard, Bishop of Durham, imprisoned by order of Henry I, who escaped from an upper window, down a rope which had been smuggled in to him.

The buildings named in italic within the text can be located on the perspective view of the Tower which appears on the centre pages.

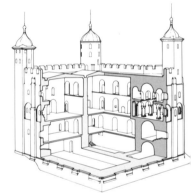

Cut-away reconstruction drawing of the White Tower as it was in the Norman period, seen from the south-west. (The modern view, on the facing page, is seen from the same angle.) At that time all the rooms on the upper floor, which were intended for royalty, rose to the roof, with a gallery at top-storey level.

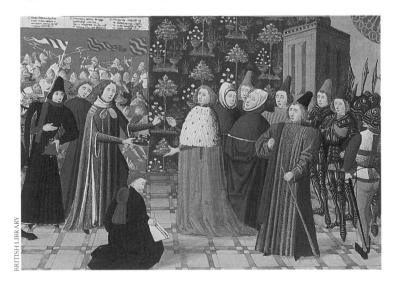

BRITISH LIBRARY

In the White Tower Richard II, condemned as a tyrant, surrenders the crown and sceptre to his cousin, Bolingbroke, who became Henry IV.

In 1244, the Welsh prince Gruffydd ap Llewelyn, a prisoner of Henry III, tried to emulate Flambard's escape but his improvised rope of knotted bed sheets came apart and he plunged to his death. In 1358, two more princely prisoners of war, the King of France, John the Good, and his son the Dauphin, were lodged in the White Tower; and after the Battle of Agincourt in 1415 Charles Duke of Orleans came there to begin his twenty-five years of imprisonment in England.

HISTORIC ROYAL PALACES

No doubt the basement of the White Tower sometimes held less fortunate anonymous captives, especially if a large batch of prisoners had to be accommodated at short notice, but these rooms were not regularly used as dungeons.

By the end of Elizabeth's reign, the White Tower had become an armoury, a storehouse for palace furnishings, and a wardrobe for royal costumes. By the eighteenth century, most of the rooms were given over to military stores and the rest to the public records, and structural changes were made which greatly altered the appearance of the building inside and out. Eventually, the military stores gave place to historic arms and armour, and the White Tower now houses part of the national collection of arms and armour in the care of the Royal Armouries.

Two princely prisoners in the White Tower. Far left *Charles, Duke of Orleans*, captured at Agincourt, was at first lodged in the old royal apartments, before being moved to a succession of English castles. Eventually, he was released on payment of a ransom. The illustration is from a manuscript edition of Orleans' poetry, dated about 1487, which was presented to Henry VII. It is the first detailed representation of the Tower. Below *The Welsh prince Gruffyd ap Llewelyn*, impatient for freedom, attempted escape in 1244 and fell to his death. This contemporary drawing by the chronicler Matthew Paris includes perhaps the earliest depiction of the Tower.

The White Tower rises 90 feet (27.4m) to the battlements and measures 118 feet (35.9 m), from east to west, by 107 feet (32.6m), north to south. The walls are 15 feet (4.6 m) thick at the base and 11 feet (3.3 m) at the top. They were built of Kentish rag, a rough limestone quarried near Maidstone. Caen stone, a finer limestone from Normandy, was used sparingly as ashlar, that is, cut stone, at the corners of the building and around door and window openings. For visual effect as well as protection from the weather, the walls were regularly whitewashed, and so the White Tower came by its name.

The Chapel of St John the Evangelist was built of the finest limestone, which had to be shipped across the Channel from Normandy. Though long since stripped of its painted decoration, the Norman stonework is little changed. The Chapel is still used occasionally for worship.

At the corners of the buildings are four turrets; three are rectangular but one, at the north-east angle, is rounded, for it contains the main spiral staircase. For a few months in 1675 this turret was used by Charles II's 'astronomical observator', John Flamsteed, before he moved to his new observatory at Greenwich. Even in Norman times the turrets probably had caps, though conical. The present cupolas date from Henry VIII's reign.

The most striking change in the outward appearance of the White Tower came with the enlargement of the windows, in 1715. Two pairs of the original Norman two-light windows remain on the top storey above the entrance. The entrance doorway now in use is the original one, set high above the ground out of reach of fire and battering ram, while the timber staircase leading up to it is a reconstruction.

The first room the visitor enters was most probably intended as the Constable's hall and the room next to it as the chamber. Originally the cross wall between was unbroken except for doorways at either end. In both rooms there are wall fireplaces, with sloping chimneys that carried the smoke out of holes higher up in the walls. The second room leads to the crypt, once the Constable's chapel.

Once, the only way up to the next floor was the turret staircase in the north-east corner. It was at the furthest possible distance from the entrance, at the opposite corner of the building, and was separated from it by the cross wall, so that even if the enemy managed to force their way through the entrance, they might still be prevented from gaining complete control of the building. The staircase now leading to the second floor was inserted later, to give direct access from the palace to St John's Chapel.

Only a few of the window openings in the White Tower survive from the Norman period. The arcading also appears around the windows at first floor level, no doubt to emphasise that this upper part of the White Tower contained the royal residence.

The Chapel of St John the Evangelist is a supreme example of early Norman church building. The pale Caen stone is undecorated save for the capitals of the columns, but is finely finished, and the overall proportions are perfect, with a careful emphasis on the rounded apse at the east end behind the altar. This severe simplicity is misleading. As a royal chapel St John's was richly decorated and furnished, with painting on the stonework, stained glass in the windows, holy images, and a painted rood screen before the altar. In 1550, as the English Reformation became truly Protestant, all these treasures were removed. Later, the Chapel housed some of the public records. When they were removed in 1857, it was even suggested that it should become an army clothing store. Instead, it was carefully restored to its original use as a place of worship.

The Chapel rises through two storeys, with a triforium on the upper level. Originally, the two adjoining rooms on this floor, once the king's great hall and his chamber, rose to the same height, each being overlooked by a gallery within the walls at the higher level. The chamber, adjoining the Chapel, contains a wall fireplace and within the wall at the end of the room, two garderobes, or lavatories. The next room, formerly the king's great hall, contains two more garderobes within the wall but no fireplace; presumably there was instead a central hearth.

On this floor and on the one below no kitchen adjoins the hall as in later castle keeps. Perhaps the cooking was done at one of the wall fireplaces or, more likely, the kitchens were outside the building, in the bailey, and the food was brought in and kept warm on braziers.

The staircase in the corner of the room passes another garderobe and leads up to the gallery which overlooked hall and chamber below and now gives on to the top floor. When this floor was inserted is not certain, but it may have been in 1603-05 when a new floor was built for a gunpowder store to serve the cannon on the roof of the White Tower.

The visitor now descends the spiral staircase within the rounded turret to the basement which contained the storerooms.

The two main rooms originally had timber ceilings, but were vaulted in brick about 1730 when the basement was used as a gunpowder store. The second main room has a well, 40 feet (12 m) deep, which still contains fresh water.

During the Peasants' Revolt of 1381 some of the rebels got into the Tower, seized the king's chief ministers, including the Archbishop of Canterbury, who had taken refuge in St John's Chapel, and beheaded them on Tower Hill.

BRITISH LIBRARY

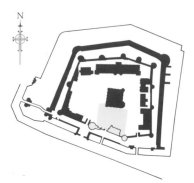

Parts of the defences of the original castle of 1066-1067 have been uncovered near the White Tower : a section of the Romans' landward *city wall*, built around AD 200, together with the foundation of a bastion built around AD400, on to which the *Wardrobe Tower* was later built, a section of the riverside city wall was built around AD390 and part of the ditch excavated by the Normans, to complete the bailey of their fort, which runs towards the Wakefield Tower.

As the castle expanded, the bailey became the inmost ward, a precinct occupied by the palace, which was bounded by the Coldharbour Gate, the Wakefield Tower, the Lanthorn Tower and the Wardrobe Tower. The *Coldharbour Gate* alone gave access to the inmost ward; only the foundations of this twin-towered gatehouse remain, adjoining the White Tower.

The *wall of the inmost ward* between the Coldharbour Gate and the Wakefield Tower remains, with its gallery of arrow loops.

The *Wakefield Tower* was built between 1220 and 1240, early in the reign of Henry III, and occupied by the king himself. It is by far the largest tower in the castle except for the White Tower, and in a sense was its successor, being at the heart of the new palace and a strongpoint in the Tower's enlarged defences, commanding on one side the main watergate, later incorporated into the Bloody Tower, and on the other side the smaller postern, the king's private entrance from the river.

DEAN AND CHAPTER, WESTMINSTER ABBEY

Henry III, from his tomb-effigy in Westminster Abbey. At the Abbey, as at the Tower, Henry renewed the work of the Norman kings.

A mason on piecework would scratch his own mark on to every stone which he had cut, so that the paymaster could reckon up what was due to him. Twenty different marks are preserved in the lower chamber of the Wakefield Tower.

The lower chamber, the guard room, overlooked the river through a line of arrow loops, until about 1280 the foreshore was built up to form the new outer ward. The arrow loops were then blocked and the floor level in the room was raised to correspond with ground level outside. This infilling has been removed to reveal the original stonework with masons' marks in perfect condition and, to complete the restoration, the original timber ceiling has been reconstructed.

The upper chamber of the Wakefield Tower, with its vaulted ceiling, large windows and fireplace, was built to be the great or bed chamber of Henry III. From the precise directions Henry gave for the decoration of the Wakefield Tower, from other surviving interiors of the period and from surviving furniture, it has been possible to give some impression of what the upper chamber may have looked like in the reign of Edward I.

HISTORIC ROYAL PALACES

HISTORIC ROYAL PALACES

The Wakefield Tower as Jewel House in 1885. Previously this room had housed part of the collection of public records at the Tower. Originally it was the king's private chamber.

HISTORIC ROYAL PALACES

The Wakefield Tower and the wall-walk along the inner curtain, seen from the wharf.

HISTORIC ROYAL PALACES

The lower chamber of the Wakefield Tower, once the guard room, has been restored to its earlier form. The excavation of the original floor level revealed stonework in perfect condition, sharply differing in colour and finish from the masonry above.

The upper chamber of the Wakefield Tower appears as it might have done during the reign of Edward I. When the king was in residence at the Tower, the room would have been enriched with wall hangings and soft furnishings.

COUNTRY LIFE PHOTOGRAPH-TOM LEIGHTON

By then it was an ante room to Edward I's new chambers in St. Thomas's Tower and was possibly used as a throne room or presence chamber. Today a throne, copied from the Coronation Chair in Westminster Abbey, can be seen. Also, facing east is a great, stained glass window lighting the king's oratory or chapel. In it can be seen the sedilia, the seat used by the priest in attendance; the piscina, the basin in which the vessels for Mass were washed and the aumbry, or wall-cupboard in which they were stored.

By tradition, the oratory is especially associated with a later king, the Lancastrian Henry VI. Taken prisoner by the new Yorkist king, Edward IV, in 1471 during the Wars of the Roses, Henry was lodged in the Wakefield Tower and shortly after was murdered, probably on Edward's order, while at prayer.

Long before Henry VI's imprisonment the Wakefield Tower had become a storehouse for official documents. After these were moved to the new Public Record Office in Chancery Lane, opened in 1856, the upper room housed the Crown Jewels until the present Jewel House opened in 1967.

Once the privy chamber in the Wakefield Tower gave access to the great chamber, where the king would meet his council or dine publicly, which in turn led to the *great hall* of the palace. The royal kitchen abutted the Wakefield Tower, and was served by a well near its present ground floor exit. Beyond the kitchen, a range of storerooms and offices backed on the wall of the inmost ward. The great hall extended up to the Lanthorn Tower After the death of Edward I in 1307, the king's private

NATIONAL PORTRAIT GALLERY

Henry VI was imprisoned and by tradition, eventually murdered, in the Wakefield Tower. Here, on the anniversary of his death, representatives of Eton College and King's College Cambridge, both of which Henry founded, lay lilies and roses on the spot where he is said to have died.

chamber was in or adjoining the Lanthorn Tower. Later the palace was enlarged: a jewel house was built against the south face of the White Tower, and an annexe on its eastern side, and eventually a second palace precinct was formed, between the Lanthorn Tower and the Wardrobe Tower on the west, and the Salt Tower and Broad Arrow Tower on the east. The medieval buildings survived long after royalty had ceased to use the palace, some being demolished in 1674-75 and others, including the great hall, incorporated into new storehouses and offices, which in turn were pulled down in 1775-77.

The original *Lanthorn Tower*, built at the same time as the Wakefield Tower, was gutted by fire in 1774 and soon after demolished. The present building is a Victorian reconstruction and contains an introduction to the inmost ward and the Medieval Palace. On display are a number of thirteenth century artefacts.

ROYAL ARMOURIES

A mid-nineteenth century engraving by George Cruikshank showing the Record Office in the Wakefield Tower, shortly before the entire collection was moved to the new Public Record Office in Chancery Lane.

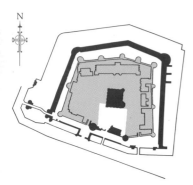

The Inner Ward lies within the curtain wall that encircles the White Tower from the Lanthorn Tower to the Wakefield Tower. Most of it, including eight wall-towers, was built in the later years of Henry III from 1238 onwards, following the completion of the palace, though his son Edward I reconstructed the western section, which includes the Beauchamp Tower, beginning in 1275.

The building of this towered curtain wall transformed the defences of the Tower. Archers and missile-throwing machines along the walls, and the towers which projected beyond them, commanded every inch of ground around the castle and could concentrate their projectiles against an attack at any point. If an enemy managed to get on to or over the wall, they were still exposed to missiles from the adjoining towers as well as from the White Tower.

Like any other castle, the Tower was rarely under attack and in normal times the wall-towers were for domestic rather than military use. Each tower occupies two or three storeys, with a sizeable chamber on each floor. These rooms together might form a suite for a resident or guest of the highest rank, accompanied by his own household, or the rooms might be arranged as self-contained accommodation.

Later on this accommodation was easily adapted to hold prisoners. Some were kept in one room, either in solitary confinement or together with their accomplices. Others, more favourably treated because of their high rank and allowed servants, were allotted an entire tower.

One such tower that can be visited today is the Salt Tower. The first floor chamber contains a fine original hooded fireplace and, beyond the staircase, a garderobe, the two essential features of a chamber fit for an occupant of high status. Indeed, one of the earliest residents in the Salt Tower, between 1297 and 1299, was John Baliol, previously King of Scotland, who had yielded his crown to Edward I following defeat in battle. In the Tudor period, this room was in constant use as a prison cell, particularly for Catholic priests during the reign of Elizabeth I. Some of their inscriptions may be seen on the walls.

A fifteenth-century town under attack. The Tower, protected by its wide moat as well as two curtain walls with flanking towers, was safe against any such assault, and none was ever attempted. Against the threat of cannon it was equipped with its own guns.

An 'aid to devotion' in the Salt Tower carved by a Catholic prisoner. It includes the names of Jesus and the Virgin Mary, and the sign of the Cross, and the Jesuit motto 'To the greater glory of God'.

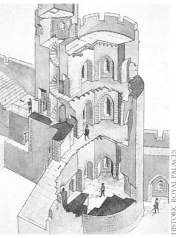

Cut-away view of the Salt Tower, as it was built about 1238, with a basement for storage, two residential rooms, and a connecting staircase. An additional floor was later inserted.

The first floor chamber of the *Broad Arrow Tower* has been set out as though occupied by Sir Simon Burley, tutor to the young Richard II who had to take refuge in the Tower during the Peasants' Revolt in 1381. Again, there is a fireplace and an adjoining garderobe.

The *Constable Tower* was largely rebuilt in the nineteenth century.

When the coronation regalia were put on show in the *Martin Tower* in 1669, they were to be seen on the ground floor, while the upper rooms became the residence of the Keeper of the Regalia. It was at this time that the mezzanine floor was built, sash windows inserted and the walls panelled. The Martin Tower was the scene of a most extraordinary episode, 'Colonel' Thomas Blood's attempt to steal the Crown Jewels, in 1671. Previously, from the Tudor period onwards, this tower had often accommodated prisoners, and a number of their inscriptions remain.

The *Brick Tower* and *Flint Tower* were rebuilt in the nineteenth century, as was the upper storey of the *Bowyer Tower*, which retains the original vaulted chamber at ground level. In the Bowyer Tower, by a plausible tradition, George Duke of Clarence, a brother of Edward IV, after his conviction for treason, was privately executed in 1478 by drowning in a butt of his favourite malmsey wine.

The *Devereux Tower*, confronting the troublesome city of London at the north-west corner of the inner ward, is of exceptional strength. It takes its name from Robert Devereux, Earl of Essex, a prisoner there at the end of Elizabeth's reign, before his execution on Tower Green nearby.

JAMES BARTHOLOMEW

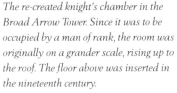
The re-created knight's chamber in the Broad Arrow Tower. Since it was to be occupied by a man of rank, the room was originally on a grander scale, rising up to the roof. The floor above was inserted in the nineteenth century.

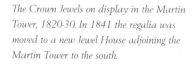
The Crown Jewels on display in the Martin Tower, 1820-30. In 1841 the regalia was moved to a new Jewel House adjoining the Martin Tower to the south.

HISTORIC ROYAL PALACES

[The Jewel House.]

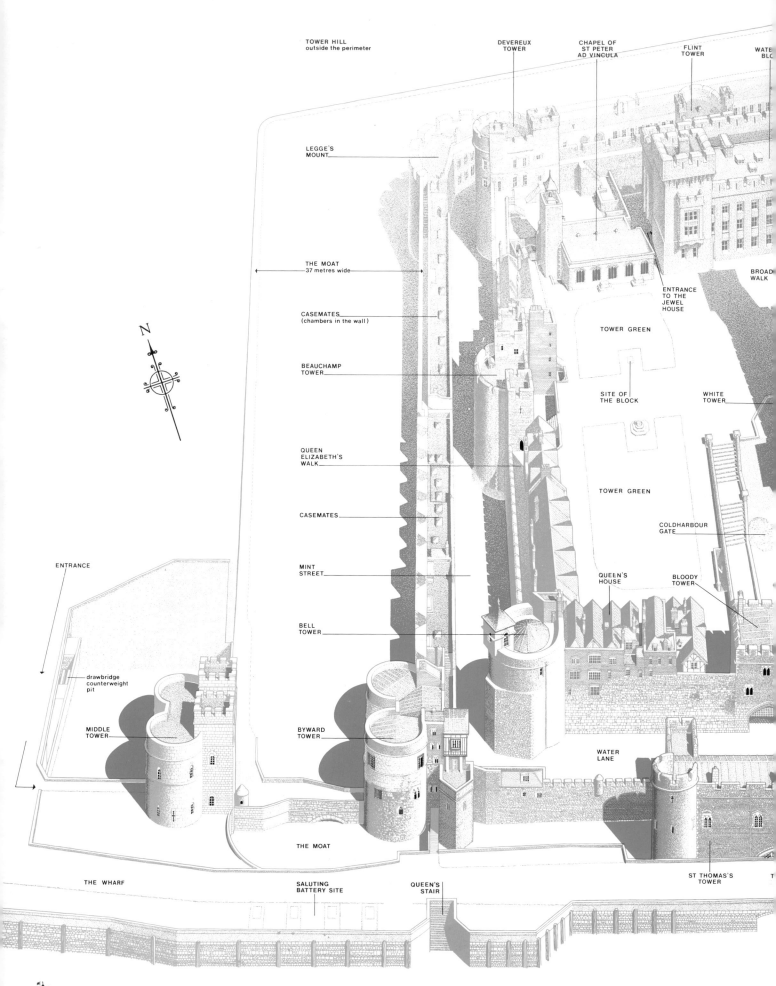

TOWER HILL
outside the perimeter

DEVEREUX
TOWER

CHAPEL OF
ST PETER
AD VINCULA

FLINT
TOWER

WATE
BLO

LEGGE'S
MOUNT

ENTRANCE
TO THE
JEWEL
HOUSE

BROAD
WALK

THE MOAT
37 metres wide

TOWER GREEN

CASEMATES
(chambers in the wall)

SITE OF
THE BLOCK

WHITE
TOWER

BEAUCHAMP
TOWER

QUEEN
ELIZABETH'S
WALK

TOWER GREEN

COLDHARBOUR
GATE

CASEMATES

MINT
STREET

QUEEN'S
HOUSE

BLOODY
TOWER

BELL
TOWER

ENTRANCE

drawbridge
counterweight
pit

MIDDLE
TOWER

BYWARD
TOWER

WATER
LANE

THE MOAT

ST THOMAS'S
TOWER

THE WHARF

SALUTING
BATTERY SITE

QUEEN'S
STAIR

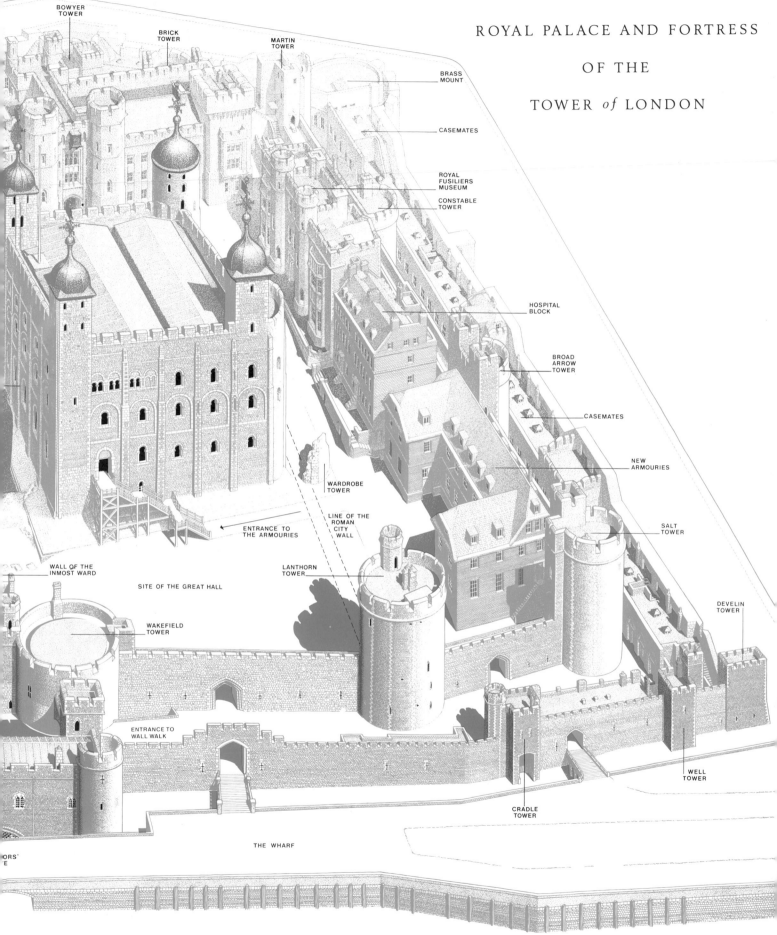

BOWYER
TOWER

BRICK
TOWER

MARTIN
TOWER

HER MAJESTY'S

ROYAL PALACE AND FORTRESS

OF THE

TOWER *of* LONDON

BRASS
MOUNT

CASEMATES

ROYAL
FUSILIERS
MUSEUM

CONSTABLE
TOWER

HOSPITAL
BLOCK

BROAD
ARROW
TOWER

CASEMATES

NEW
ARMOURIES

SALT
TOWER

DEVELIN
TOWER

WARDROBE
TOWER

LINE OF THE
ROMAN CITY
WALL

ENTRANCE TO
THE ARMOURIES

WALL OF THE
INMOST WARD

SITE OF THE GREAT HALL

LANTHORN
TOWER

WAKEFIELD
TOWER

ENTRANCE TO
WALL WALK

WELL
TOWER

CRADLE
TOWER

THE WHARF

The *Beauchamp Tower*, built by Edward I in about 1281, replaced the twin-towered gatehouse of Henry III's time which had controlled the landward entrance to his castle across the moat, and actually incorporated the foundations of the earlier building. The interior of the Beauchamp Tower reveals the extensive use of brick, a notable feature of Edward I's work at the Tower and, on this scale, an innovation in English castle-building.

Along the entire length of the adjoining curtain wall, from the Devereux Tower to the Bell Tower, ran a gallery with embrasures and arrow loops through which archers could command the outer defences towards the city. When only a few years later the outer curtain wall was heightened above the level of the loops, this elaborate arrangement was made useless.

The Beauchamp Tower takes its name from Thomas Beauchamp, Earl of Warwick, whom Richard II imprisoned in it from 1397 to 1399. With ample accommodation for a nobleman and his household within its three storeys, and under the eye of the Constable or his deputy residing nearby, where Queen's House now stands, the Beauchamp Tower was especially suitable for prisoners of high rank. In Mary I's reign, John Dudley, Duke of Northumberland, and his five sons were held here; in Elizabeth I's reign Philip Howard, Earl of Arundel, died within its walls; and here Lord Cobham spent the last fourteen years of his life in the reign of James I.

The *Bell Tower* and the adjoining curtain wall up to the Bloody Tower date from the first enlargement of the Tower in the 1190s; at that time they stood on the edge of the river. The Bell Tower was

The Beauchamp Tower dominates the western defences of the Tower, facing the city. They are the work of Edward I's reign, between 1275 and 1285.

This elaborate family memorial in the Beauchamp Tower was carved, no doubt by a hired craftsman, for John Dudley, eldest son of the Duke of Northumberland, while he and his four brothers were prisoners of Mary I. The Duke had tried to exclude Mary from the throne in favour of Lady Jane Grey, his daughter-in-law. The lion and bear are family emblems; the various flowers represent the names of John's brothers.

The Bell Tower, with Queen's House adjoining, from the wharf.

supported by a rubble platform, and its solid base, 16 feet (5 m) high, was protected at ground level by a stepped plinth. The tower was probably built in two phases, the original polygonal shape being changed at the second storey to a circular plan. The curfew bell has been rung from this tower for at least 500 years: the present bell dates from 1651.

Princess Elizabeth, the future Elizabeth I, at the age of 13. Five years later she was held prisoner in the upper room of the Bell Tower, while she was questioned about her knowledge of plots against her half-sister Mary I. After two months, Elizabeth was released, but retained a lasting dislike of the Tower and as queen returned only once, briefly, before her coronation.

Probably from the beginning the Constable's house adjoined the Bell Tower, so that the officer in command of the castle should reside at this key point in its defences, facing the river and the city. Under the Tudors, when a major responsibility of the Constable's resident deputy, the Lieutenant, was the safekeeping of prisoners, the Bell Tower became the lodging of captives of the highest importance, such as Sir Thomas More, Princess Elizabeth (the future Elizabeth I), Arabella Stuart, cousin of James I, and perhaps also the Duke of Monmouth, natural son of Charles II.

Before the building of St Thomas's Tower, the gatetower which was to become the *Bloody Tower* controlled the watergate. After that it gave access from the outer ward to the inner ward. The upper stage of the present tower was largely reconstructed in the reign of Edward III, about 1360. The first floor contains the windlass that still operates the portcullis at the front of the gatehall below. Originally, there was a second portcullis, worked from the other side of the room. The room was intended to be superior accommodation, perhaps a guest chamber or office for the use of the Constable who lived nearby. It contains a good fireplace, a large side window which once had window seats, and a floor covered with richly decorated tiles. Eventually this tower was to accommodate such eminent prisoners as two Archbishops of Canterbury, Thomas Cranmer (in 1553-54) and William Laud (in 1640-45), and a Lord Chancellor, Jeffreys of the 'Bloody Assizes'(in 1688-89).

Sir Thomas More, once Henry VIII's chancellor, was imprisoned in the lower room of the Bell Tower for fifteen months, in increasingly harsh conditions, but still refused to acknowledge the King as head of the English Church in place of the Pope. Finally, More was convicted of treason and beheaded on Tower Hill.

The portcullis and its machinery in the Bloody Tower, probably dating from the Tudor period and still in working order.

Once known as the Garden Tower, since it adjoined the Lieutenant's garden, this tower at some time in the Tudor period came to be called the Bloody Tower, because (so James I was told when he visited the Tower in 1604) it was there that the 'Princes in the Tower' had been murdered.

The princes, twelve-year-old Edward and his younger brother, the sons of Edward IV, had been lodged in the Tower, following their father's death in 1483, under the protection of their uncle, Richard Duke of Gloucester. Preparations began for Edward's coronation but in the event it was their uncle who was crowned in his place as Richard III. The princes remained in the Tower for a time and then were lost to view. Much has been written about their fate, largely in order to prove or disprove Richard's complicity in their deaths, but no conclusive evidence has been produced on either side. Even the bones of two children found buried close to the White Tower in 1674, which were officially reburied in Westminster Abbey as the remains of the princes, cannot be positively identified.

Certainly there have been two authenticated cases of violent death within the Bloody Tower. In 1585 the 8th Earl of Northumberland shot himself to escape conviction for treason and the forfeiture of his family lands to Elizabeth I. In James I's reign, in scandalous circumstances which touched even the King himself, Sir Thomas Overbury was poisoned while a prisoner there.

The Bloody Tower is now furnished as it might have appeared during the thirteen-year imprisonment (1603-16) of Sir Walter Ralegh by James I. Indeed, to allow Ralegh and his family more living space, the tower was heightened and a new floor inserted, making the present upper chamber.

Adjoining the Bell Tower, in the south-west corner of the inner ward, stands an L-shaped, timber-framed Tudor building, originally known as the Lieutenant's Lodgings. Its present name *Queen's House*, dates from Queen Victoria's reign, and changes according to whether the sovereign is king or queen. Queen's House is now occupied by the Resident Governor, the Lieutenant's successor as officer with local command of the Tower. It is not open to the public.

Many prisoners of high rank were lodged there, under the personal supervision of the Lieutenant, the first, by Tower tradition, being Anne Boleyn, the second of Henry VIII's six wives to be followed five years later by his fifth wife, Catherine Howard. In the Council Chamber on the upper floor of Queen's House is an elaborate contemporary memorial commemorating the discovery of the Gunpowder Plot in 1605, which followed the examination in this room of Guy Fawkes before and after torture.

One prisoner in the Lieutenant's care managed to take his leave unknown to his host the night before he was to be executed. The Scottish Jacobite Earl of Nithsdale, captured after the defeat of the 1715 rebellion, escaped from Queen's House, rouged and in woman's clothing which had been smuggled in by his indomitable wife.

Sir Thomas Overbury had tried in vain to dissuade his friend the Earl of Somerset from marrying the evil Frances Howard. In revenge, she used her husband's influence with the King, James I, to have Overbury imprisoned in the Bloody Tower, and finally contrived his murder by poison.

In this room, the lower chamber of the Bloody Tower, Sir Walter Ralegh wrote a History of the World *for the instruction of Henry Prince of Wales, while a prisoner of his father James I. The portrait depicts Ralegh at the height of his greatness, as favourite of Elizabeth I and captain of her bodyguard.*

Right *The Princes in the Tower fearfully await their end, as depicted by the Victorian painter John Millais. The darker side of the Tower's history, so rich in pathos and horror, fascinated the Victorians, the poignant figures of the Princes and of Lady Jane Grey being especially popular.*

The axe, which is of the Tudor period, was for long displayed at the Tower as the instrument of Anne Boleyn's death, although in fact by her own choice she was beheaded with a sword. The block was made for the last beheading on Tower Hill in 1747.

By tradition, Anne Boleyn stayed in Queen's House, before her execution on Tower Green for the crime of adulterous treason. Of all the Tower ghosts, Anne's has been most often reported, beneath the window of the room in which she is said to have spent her last days.

Robert Devereux, Earl of Essex, the last victim of the axe on Tower Green in 1601. Having lost the favour of Elizabeth I, he had tried to raise a rebellion and overthrow his rivals at court by force.

Queen's House, formerly the Lieutenant's Lodgings, was built in Henry VIII's last years. Distinguished prisoners were housed there in the Lieutenant's keeping or dined at his table.

The last prisoner to be given accommodation in Queen's House was Rudolf Hess, the Deputy Fuhrer of Nazi Germany, for four days in May 1941.

On the other side of Tower Green seven notable prisoners were executed. The first was William, Lord Hastings, in 1483, hurriedly beheaded after his arrest at a meeting of the royal council in the White Tower at the instance of the Protector, Richard of Gloucester. The next five victims were the only women to suffer death by beheading for treason. Anne Boleyn and Catherine Howard, Henry's fifth wife, had both been convicted of adultery. Jane, Viscountess Rochford, Catherine's lady-in-waiting, was implicated in her crime. One offence of the aged Margaret Pole, Countess of Salisbury, in the eyes of the Tudor Henry VIII, was her Yorkist blood, just as Lady Jane Grey, a victim of her cousin, Mary I, suffered for her descent from Henry VII which made her, despite herself, a rival to Mary. These women were all spared public execution on Tower Hill, the customary place for beheadings, to avoid embarrassing them as well as the monarch. The last of the seven, the Earl of Essex, the young favourite of Elizabeth I, may have been singled out for the same reason, although the Queen's ministers were more concerned with Essex's dangerous popularity among the Londoners and no doubt feared what might happen if he were taken out to Tower Hill.

The *Chapel Royal of St Peter ad Vincula*, close by the scaffold site, is the last resting place of all those who died there and also of many who died on Tower Hill. The dedication to St Peter 'in chains' suggests a special association with prisoners but long predates the time when the Tower came into regular use as a prison. St Peter's had been a city parish church standing outside the Tower which was incorporated into the castle when it was enlarged by Henry III. He had the Chapel richly furnished and decorated as the place of worship for the general population of the Tower, the Chapel of St John in the White Tower being restricted to the sovereign and his court. St Peter's was rebuilt in the reign of Henry's son, Edward I, and again rebuilt, in its present form, in 1519-20, in the early years of Henry VIII's reign. It is therefore a rare example of early Tudor church architecture, consisting of a nave and chancel and an equally wide north aisle, both with tie-beam roofs of Spanish chestnut.

The Chapel contains some splendid monuments com- memorating officers of the Tower, their wives, and families, as well as memorials to many humble residents of the Tower who worshipped in this their parish church, but it is known above all

Margaret Pole, Countess of Salisbury, was beheaded on Tower Green at the age of 70 by order of Henry VIII. The King had come to see the Poles as a focus of conspiracies against him because of their royal descent from the House of York and loyalty to the Catholic religion.

Lady Jane Grey at the age of 16 became the 'Nine Days' Queen'. Brought to the Tower to await her coronation, she remained as the prisoner of her successful rival Mary I in the house of the Gentleman Gaoler, until her execution a few yards away on Tower Green.

The nave and chancel of the Chapel of St Peter ad Vincula. Almost completely rebuilt early in Henry VIII's reign, the Chapel is the final resting place of his most famous victims.

as the burial place of some of the most celebrated Tower prisoners including three queens, Anne Boleyn, Catherine Howard and Jane Grey – the uncrowned 'Nine Days' Queen' – and many others of noble blood or high position including two saints of the Roman Catholic Church, Sir Thomas More and Bishop John Fisher. At the time, their headless bodies were buried hastily and carelessly, without any memorial, under the nave or chancel. When, with Queen Victoria's approval, the Chapel was restored in 1876, the remains unearthed in the nave, along with some intact coffins, were re-interred in the crypt. Bones found in the chancel, some of which could be identified, including the remains of Anne Boleyn, were reburied beneath the marble pavement before the altar. From that time the Chapel has held regular church services which are open to the public. The fine organ built by Bernhardt Schmidt for the Banqueting House at Whitehall in 1699, and adorned with carvings by Grinling Gibbons, was installed in 1890. In 1966 a professional choir which has won a notable reputation was established. Visitors may enter the Chapel only with a Yeoman Warder's tour, which they may be allowed to join outside on Tower Green.

John Fisher, Bishop of Rochester, like his friend, Sir Thomas More, died for the unity of the Catholic church under the Pope. Both were canonised in 1935. Drawing by Holbein.

Gargoyle on the Victorian Gothic Waterloo Barracks.

The *Waterloo Block* (formally Barracks), with accommodation for almost 1000 men, was built while the Duke of Wellington was Constable of the Tower, in a castellated neo-Gothic style complete with elaborate battlements and gargoyles. Since 1967, the Crown Jewels have been housed at the western end of the Waterloo Barracks, near the Chapel of St Peter ad Vincula.

Next to the Waterloo Barracks, and in similar style, was the Officers' Mess, now the Headquarters of the Royal Regiment of Fusiliers. It also contains the *Royal Fusiliers Museum*, for which there is a separate admission charge. The Fusiliers' connection with the Tower goes back to the formation of the Regiment here in 1685, initially to guard the Tower's guns.

The houses next to the Fusiliers' Headquarters were built in 1699-1700. Originally they were occupied by officials of the Board of Ordnance. Later they became the *Hospital Block* for the Tower garrison.

The *New Armouries*, also built for the Ordnance, in 1663-64, is now occupied by the Royal Armouries.

HISTORIC ROYAL PALACES

Not only victims of the axe but many Tower residents were buried within the Chapel or in the adjoining cemetery. One of several remarkable funeral monuments commemorates Sir Richard Blount and his son Sir Michael Blount, both Lieutenants of the Tower in the reign of Elizabeth I, together with their families.

HISTORIC ROYAL PALACES

The Chapel Royal of St Peter ad Vincula is also the parish church of the Tower where Sunday services regularly take place, as well as christenings and weddings in the families of those who live and work there.

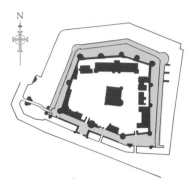

The outer ward was created by Edward I's expansion of the Tower in 1275-85. On the landward side it was originally bounded by a low retaining wall on the edge of the new moat. Soon after, this outer curtain was built up not far short of its present height. It was still low enough, however, for defenders on the inner walls and towers to aim and shoot across the moat and command the outer wall should it fall to an enemy.

At the north-west and north-east corners of the outer ward were rounded bastions, from which archers might cover the moat as well as the high ground of Tower Hill. In 1683 the bastions were converted into gun emplacements, from which time date their present names of *Legge's Mount* and *Brass Mount*.

HISTORIC ROYAL PALACES. PHOTOGRAPH: EARL BEESLEY

Midway between Legge's Mount and Brass Mount, the smaller North Bastion was built in 1848, at the time of the Chartist agitation, against the threat of mob attack. This last significant addition to the Tower's defences was destroyed by a bomb in the Second World War.

Much of the area between the inner and outer curtain walls, from the Bell Tower round to the Salt Tower, was eventually occupied by the workshops, offices, and houses of the Royal Mint, and the section north of the Bell Tower is still known as Mint Street. The Victorian cottages ranged against the outer wall, called the *Casemates*, are now the homes of most of the Yeoman Warders of the Tower and their families.

St Thomas's Tower, built between 1275 and 1279, during Edward I's enlargement of the Tower. The timber framing above the great arch behind Traitors' Gate is Tudor, dating from 1532-33.

On the river front the outer ward still bears the name of *Water Lane*, recalling that it was constructed upon the foreshore of the river. The main watergate giving access to the outer ward was below *St Thomas's Tower*, built by Edward I between 1275 and 1279 to replace Henry III's royal apartments in the Wakefield Tower. Facing the river . . . dedicated to St Thomas (Thomas Becket). The hall has been reconstructed and the oratory re-glazed with coloured glass. The chamber next door has been left unrestored to show the degree to which the buildings have been altered since the thirteenth century.

Legge's Mount, one of the two medieval bastions overlooking Tower Hill, which were rebuilt to include gun ports in 1683.

The coining presses in the Tower Mint, depicted by Thomas Rowlandson in 1809. Until 1662 the Tower Mint struck coins by hand. Then presses were introduced and continued in use until the Mint was moved out in 1811-12, to a new building on Tower Hill where steam-powered machinery was installed.

In 1993, after major restoration, St Thomas's Tower was opened to the public for the first time. The king's aula, or hall, (left) has been reconstructed to show what it might have looked like in the reign of Edward I.

TRAITORS' GATE

TIM MERCER

In 1532, in preparation for the coronation of Anne Boleyn, St Thomas's Tower was largely rebuilt to provide apartments for high-ranking court officials. Meanwhile, through the watergate below, Traitors' Gate, passed the increasing flow of prisoners of state that began after Henry's break with Rome.

By the early eighteenth century, the status and condition of St Thomas's Tower had sadly deteriorated. In the pool behind Traitors' Gate was an engine worked originally either by the tide or horses, and eventually by steam power, which raised water to a cistern on the roof of the White Tower; it could also be adapted to drive machinery for boring gun barrels. The boring room was inside St Thomas's Tower which, as well as the Keeper of the Engine, accommodated a number of Yeoman Warders and the patients of the Tower infirmary.

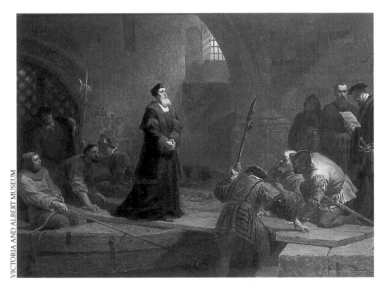

VICTORIA AND ALBERT MUSEUM

'Cranmer at the Traitors' Gate', by Frederick Goodall, 1856. The sombre scene of a prisoner's arrival was depicted in many Victorian paintings and engravings. The venerable Thomas Cranmer, who had served Henry VIII and his son Edward VI as Archbishop of Canterbury, had obeyed Edward's last wishes and supported the attempt to place the Protestant Lady Jane Grey on the throne.

Beneath St Thomas's Tower Edward I had built a new private entrance for royalty arriving by river. In Edward III's reign, after the royal apartments came to be in or near the Lanthorn Tower, a private watergate was built for the king at the *Cradle Tower* between 1348 and 1355.

The *Well Tower* is perhaps the only tower other than the White Tower to have kept its original name, for though it did not have a well its outer wall contained chutes down which buckets were lowered into the river.

The *Develin Tower*, at the south-east corner of the outer ward, at one period led to a causeway across the moat. The main landward entrance into the outer ward was at the western end, by way of the Byward Tower.

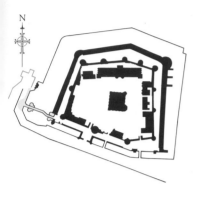

The *Byward Tower* was the innermost of three gate-towers which defended the entrance across the moat. The sequence of defences encountered by an enemy advancing towards the Byward Tower comprised a drawbridge in the causeway, arrow loops in the twin towers on each side of the gatehall, a portcullis with 'murder holes' in the outer arch (down which might come not only missiles but also water to quench a fire), then the gates, and finally a second portcullis. All these defences are still in place, except for the drawbridge and the inner portcullis. The room above the gatehall, not open to the public, contains the portcullis winding-gear and also the only painted decoration which survives in the Tower from the Middle Ages, a Crucifixion scene, dating from about 1400, which has lacked the figure of Christ at its centre since a fireplace was inserted when the room was remodelled in the Tudor period. The timber framing at the back of the tower was rebuilt at the same time. Between the gatehall of the Byward Tower and the Water Lane shop is the entrance to the postern tower which gave access from the wharf by a drawbridge. After the Cradle Tower was cut off from the river by the extension of the wharf, the postern at the Byward Tower became the entrance for royalty and other distinguished visitors coming to the Tower by water. The stairs at which they landed beside the wharf are now known as Queen's Stairs.

The *Middle Tower* is of similar design to the Byward Tower. Although partly re-faced with Portland stone in 1717 it contains many original features. The royal arms above the outer arch are those of George I, then the reigning monarch.

The western entrance, through the Middle Tower (right) and Byward Tower. Once the Middle Tower was in the middle, between the Byward Tower and the now vanished Lion Tower, while the Byward Tower remains 'by the ward', that is, the outer ward.

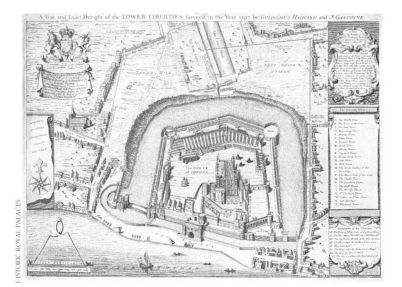

This view, dated 1597, shows the medieval defences at the main entrance, including the outwork on Tower Hill, called the Bulwark, and the barbican, known as the Lion Tower, which controlled the first section of the causeway across the moat. Only the buried foundations of these buildings remain.

Only the foundations of the Lion Tower remain, marked out by a semicircle of stones set in the cobbles. A drawbridge linked the Lion Tower to the further side of the moat; below the modern walkway is the pit into which the weighted end of the bridge fell. The Lion Tower took its name from the royal menagerie, famous for its lions, which once was housed nearby on the wharf but was later moved into the Lion Tower itself. There it remained, although a serious impediment to traffic in and out of the Tower, until the menagerie was closed in 1834, when

World War Two allotments in the Tower moat. After the moat had been drained it became a training ground for the soldiers stationed at the Tower. It is now used for the recreation of Tower residents, with a bowling green in one corner and a tennis court and playground in another.

some of the animals were taken to the new zoo which had been formed at Regent's Park.

As an additional defence of this entrance, a large brick outwork on the further side of the moat, called the Bulwark, was built by Edward IV in about 1480, after the Wars of the Roses.

The excavation of the moat, the work of Edward I's reign, took some six years. It was filled from the river at high tide; sluice gates held in the water as the river ebbed, and controlled the flow in order to work tide-mills. Eventually, the moat was cut off from the river, and its stagnant waters filled up with refuse from the Tower and the houses on Tower Hill. In 1843, after several outbreaks of cholera in the Tower, the moat was drained and filled in to about the previous water level.

TOWER WHARF

When the Tower was the chief storehouse of armaments in the country, much of the wharf was taken up with the movement and storage of munitions, and it accommodated at different times cannon-foundries, a small arms factory and proof yard. The wharf also had a ceremonial role as the landing-place of royalty and of foreign dignitaries before they entered the city, while ever since the time of Henry VIII who first had the Tower well defended with ordnance, the guns along the wharf have been fired on occasions of national rejoicing. Royal salutes are nowadays fired from the gunpark, at the western end of the wharf.

As the artillery at the Tower is part of the Royal Armouries collection, the guns for salutes are brought in by a detachment of the Honourable Artillery Company, towing four 25-pounders behind Landrovers. Sixty-two gun salutes are fired for royal occasions, on the anniversaries of the birthdays, actual and official, of the Queen, of the Queen's accession, and of the birthdays of Prince Philip and the Queen Mother. Forty-one guns are fired at the State Opening of Parliament and when a foreign Head of State arrives on an official visit to the Queen.

Simon Fraser, Lord Lovat, the last of the rebel Scottish lords to be executed after the Jacobite rebellion of 1745, became a London celebrity while awaiting trial. His death on Tower Hill in 1747, at the age of 80, was the last beheading to take place in Britain. It concluded triumphantly, an onlooker reported, with 'a prodigious stroke' by the headsman that left 'the axe near two inches in the block'. Portrait by William Hogarth.

Previous page The arrival of Venetian Ambassadors at the Tower Stairs, May 1707, by the Venetian painter Luca Carlevaris.

The firing of a royal salute by the Honourable Artillery Company from Tower wharf.

TOWER HILL

Most of Tower Hill was once part of the Liberties of the Tower, the area outside the walls which was nonetheless under the jurisdiction of the Tower and independent of the City of London. The Liberties are now marked by 31 boundary-stones, each bearing the broad arrow denoting royal ownership, from Tower Pier around the Hill and down by St Katharine's Way to

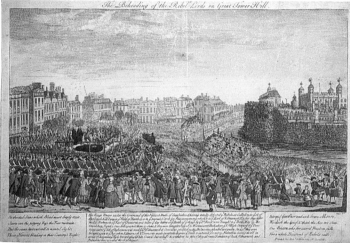

When the Earl of Kilmarnock and Lord Balmerino were executed for their part in the 1745 rebellion, a troop of lifeguards and 1000 footguards were stationed around the scaffold, to hold back the vast crowds. A Tower Hill execution was one of the great popular spectacles of London.

the Iron Gate Stairs by Tower Bridge. Every third year, on Ascension Day, the Tower's authority is re-asserted in the ceremony of Beating the Bounds.

The Tower Hill postern, the foundations of which are at the end of the subway leading to the underground station, was built soon after the completion of the new moat, around 1300, in effect as part of the Tower's defences. The postern gave entrance through the city wall, a section of which survives beyond the underpass.

On the other side of the roadway, in Trinity Gardens, lies the marked site of the scaffold on Tower Hill. Some 125 Tower prisoners died there, most by beheading which was the honourable form of execution allowed to nobles and gentlemen found guilty of treason. Their deaths were watched by unruly crowds numbering many thousands. Viewing stands were put up around the scaffold, and sometimes collapsed under the weight of eager spectators.

Traitors of lowlier status suffered death by hanging, drawing and quartering, sometimes on the Hill but most often at Tyburn, near the site of Marble Arch. Not all who died on Tower Hill were convicted traitors. Some were burned as heretics, and others hanged as common criminals, as were the last of those to be executed on this spot, in 1780.

Local choirboys armed with willow wands beat the bounds of the Tower Liberties. The ceremony dates back at least to 1381.

One of the boundary-stones marking the limits of the Tower Liberties.

THE ROYAL ARMOURIES

Japanese armour, of about 1610, sent to King James I by the Governor of Edo (Tokyo) in 1614. It was restored by Japanese craftsmen in 1972.

The Royal Armouries derives from the great arsenal at the Tower which supplied armour and weapons to the medieval English kings and their armies. The present collection took shape in the reign of Henry VIII who re-stocked the Tower arsenal, and also set up a workshop at Greenwich to make fine armour for himself and his court. Henry's armours, and those of the early Stuarts, were eventually brought together at the Tower, and early in Charles II's reign the historic collection was opened to the public, along with artillery and weapon-stores of the working arsenal.

Subsequently the Tower Armouries were enriched by the return of obsolete weapons to store, and by the quickening inflow of the spoils of British conquests in every part of the world. As the scholarly study of arms and armour developed in the 19th century, a systematic attempt began to fill in the gaps in the inherited collections.

At the present time, European armour and weapons, ranging from the age of the Saxons and Vikings up to the modern times, are displayed in the White Tower and New Armouries. Some pieces from the Royal Armouries Oriental collection as well as the instruments of torture and punishment are also on view in the White Tower.

Presentation sabre of Sir William Fenwick Williams, decorated by the French goldsmith Antoine Vechte, 1856.

The display includes arms and armour for war, for the tournament, for hunting, for self-defence and for display and fashion, each type designed carefully for its particular purpose. There are striking examples of technological innovation and ingenuity, and fine works of art created for wealthy patrons. As well as the Tudor and Stuart royal armours, still the centrepiece of the collections, the visitor will also encounter many exhibits of immediate appeal: armours for a giant and a dwarf, and for children, and for horses; gunshields and combination weapons; fearsome staff weapons and elegant rapiers; and the arsenal displays in the vaults of the White Tower.

Right Foot combat armour of Henry VIII, part of a garniture, or set, of armours for war and the tournament, made for the King in 1540 at the royal armour workshops which he had established at Greenwich Palace.

Far right Dutch gilt parade armour of Charles I, probably made for his elder brother Henry Prince of Wales, and inherited by Charles on his death in 1612.

Below German wheellock pistol, made about 1580: the barrel and lockplate etched and gilt, the stock inlaid with staghorn, the ball of the stock decorated with copper-gilt engraved bands and lions' masks.

ROYAL ARMOURIES

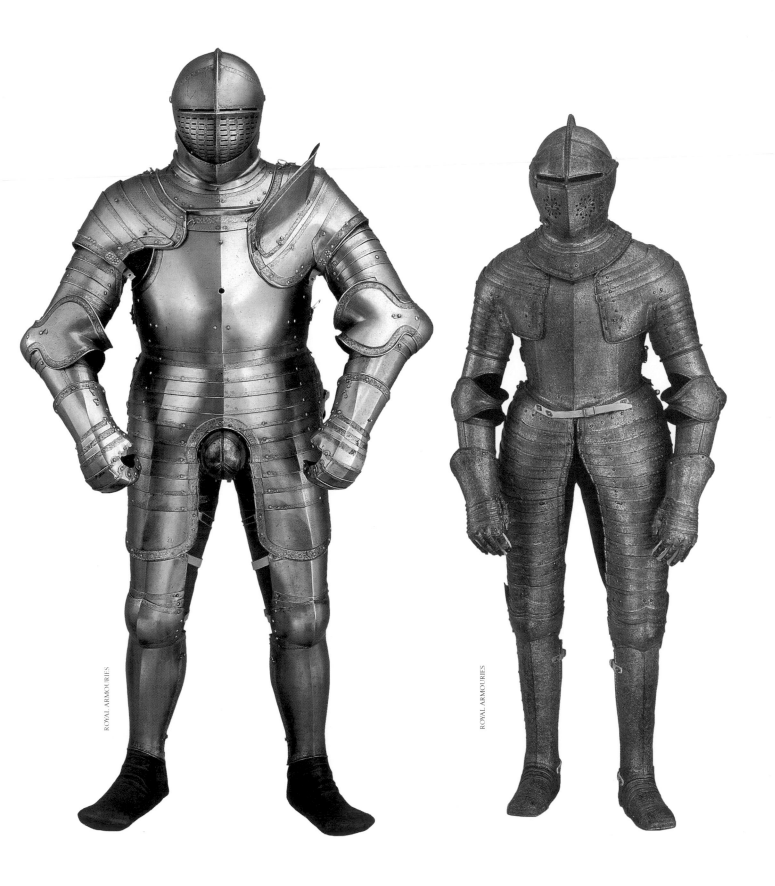

THE CROWN JEWELS

The Tower of London was one of the chief treasuries of the medieval kings, and some of the Crown Jewels were always kept there. The coronation regalia, however, which were regarded as the relics of St Edward (King Edward the Confessor, who ruled before the Norman Conquest) were kept at Westminster Abbey, where the royal saint was buried and coronations took place.

Following the execution of Charles I in 1649, Parliament ordered the coronation ornaments to be brought to the Tower, the precious metals to be melted down for coinage, and the gems sold off. Nevertheless, several of the old regalia, or parts of them, reappeared and were refashioned for use at Charles II's coronation in 1661. The lower half at least of the coronation crown itself was made up of a medieval crown, perhaps the crown of Edward the Confessor.

Later monarchs added to the regalia, most notably the Jewelled State Sword made for the coronation of George IV in 1821, and the Imperial State Crown with which Queen Victoria was crowned in 1837. The major gemstones set in the crown, however, had a much longer history, including a sapphire taken from the ring said to have been buried with Edward the Confessor in 1066, and the balas ruby presented to the Black Prince in 1367.

The Anointing Spoon, the oldest piece of the regalia, dates from the twelfth century; the handle at least may have been used at the coronation of King John.

The Jewelled State Sword made for George IV, with its scabbard of solid gold decorated with diamonds, emeralds, and rubies in the form of roses, thistles and shamrocks, the emblems of England, Scotland and Ireland.

As well as the coronation ornaments and robes, a number of historic crowns are displayed, including the Crown of Queen Elizabeth the Queen Mother, which holds the legendary Koh-i-noor diamond.

The Jewel House also contains banqueting and church plate, state swords, processional maces and trumpets, the robes and insignia of the orders of chivalry, and decorations and medals.

An illustrated guidebook to the Crown Jewels is on sale in the Tower shops.

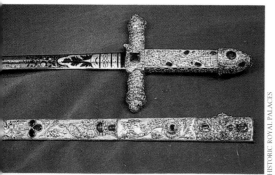

The body of the eagle Ampulla, which is used to contain the holy oil with which the new monarch is anointed, was made for Charles II's coronation in 1661, but the head can be dated to the fourteenth century.

HISTORIC ROYAL PALACES

The Imperial State Crown, worn by the monarch at major state occasions, is encrusted with more than 2800 small diamonds, and set with several historic gemstones as well as the Second Star of Africa, one of the nine major stones cut from the Cullinan Diamond.

St Edward's Crown, used only at a coronation, may indeed date back to Edward the Confessor, for the accounts of Charles II's goldsmith show that he must have used one of the medieval crowns, perhaps the Confessor's, adding to it the arches, monde, and cross.

The head of the Sceptre with the Cross, which was made for Charles II, now contains the Star of Africa, at 530 carats the largest cut diamond in the world.

HISTORIC ROYAL PALACES

HISTORIC ROYAL PALACES

THE COMMUNITY *of* THE TOWER

Once the Tower must have contained as many as a thousand inhabitants. Nowadays, some 150 people live within its walls, chiefly the Yeoman Warders and resident Tower officers and their families.

From some time early in the Tower's history, the custody of the gates and the safekeeping of prisoners were entrusted to a body of warders headed by a porter appointed directly by the king. From the reign of Henry VIII these duties were carried out by a body of the king's yeomen at the Tower, who were accounted members of the royal guard and were entitled to wear the royal

The body of Yeoman Warders drawn up on Tower Green at the installation of a new Constable of the Tower.

livery, like the Yeomen of the Guard who attended the person of the monarch.

Both the Yeoman Warders of the Tower and the Yeomen of the Guard are popularly known as 'Beefeaters', but the nickname was first given to the latter as early as the seventeenth century, when indeed any well fed domestic retainer might be called a 'beefeater'.

Nowadays, there are about 40 Yeoman Warders, who are former warrant officers in the Army, Royal Marines or Royal Air Force, with an honourable service record of at least 22 years.

The Tower guard is detached for duty at the Tower from the same regiment which provides the guard at Buckingham Palace and St James's Palace, usually one of the five regiments of Foot Guards. When one detachment replaces another, the ceremonial changing of the guard takes place on Tower Green.

At the conclusion of the Ceremony of the Keys, after the locking of the gates, the Chief Yeoman Warder and his escort encounter the main Tower guard, who present arms. The Chief Warder, raising his bonnet, calls 'God preserve Queen Elizabeth', and the guard and escort respond 'Amen'. Then the Last Post echoes round Tower Green.

By tradition, there have been ravens at the Tower from its very beginnings, when these scavengers flew in to feed off the abundant refuse of the castle. Their presence has been protected by the legend that without its ravens the Tower will fall and the kingdom with it. Nowadays, their wings are clipped to prevent them straying. Normally replacement birds are brought to the Tower from Scotland, Wales or the west of England. However, in recent years some have been hatched at the Tower. Ravens are long-lived, averaging 25 years.

There are usually six ravens in residence, cared for by one of the Yeoman Warders, with the title of Ravenmaster. The ravens' cage is near the Wakefield Tower, and their cemetery is in the moat between the Middle Drawbridge and St Thomas's Tower.

Of all the traditions and ceremonies of the Tower one above all evokes its essential character as a royal palace and fortress, the nightly Ceremony of the Keys (open to the public by application in advance). The outer gates of the fortress are locked and the keys taken to the monarch's representative in the

Tower, the Resident Governor. Then, for a few hours, the Tower reverts to its original condition, a community separate and secure, until next morning the gates are unlocked and this great national showplace is once more open to the world.

*The Chief Yeoman Warder's
mace of office.*